D0611058

A Special Gift

presented to:

Mommy

from:

Evan

date:

May 6, 2002

a little book of

hugs™

for *Mom*

Inspiration for the Heart

HOWARD
PUBLISHING CO.

A Little Book of Hugs for Mom
© 2000 by Howard Publishing Co., Inc.
All rights reserved. Printed in China

Published by Howard Publishing Co., Inc.,
3117 North 7th Street, West Monroe, LA 71291-2227

00 01 02 03 04   5 4 3 2 1

ISBN: 1-58229-119-5

Messages by G. A. Myers
Paraphrased Scriptures by LeAnn Weiss
Interior design by LinDee Loveland and Vanessa Bearden
Project Editor: Philis Boultinghouse

CONTENTS

I remember, I remember
The house where
I was born
The little window
where the sun
Came peeping in at morn.

—THOMAS HOOD

CHAPTER ONE

a Mother's Love

*Cultivate faith, goodness,
knowledge, self-control,
perseverance, godliness,*

brotherly kindness, and love
in your children. For if they
are growing in these qualities,
they won't be ineffective or
unproductive, and they will
never stumble.

Love,
Your Living God

2 Peter 1:5–11

You may not realize it, but you are a gifted gardener. Though you may be incapable of keeping a simple houseplant alive, you are an accomplished gardener nonetheless.

*B*ut the soil you
work in is not of
this world. No! It
is the soil of the
human heart.

*Y*our children are your
fertile field, and in their
hearts you have planted
your seeds of love, joy,
peace, patience, kindness,
goodness, faithfulness,
gentleness, and
self-control.

*Y*ou have courageously
protected your precious
field from destructive and
uninvited strangers.
When spiritual or physical
disease threatened, you
worked with bleeding
hands to free the roots of
life from contaminants.

17

*Y*ou have nursed the wounds left by the violent storms of life. You have struggled through seasons of drought; you have celebrated at the sight of unhampered growth.

*Y*ou have weeded,
watered, plowed,
and prayed.

In turn, you should know that your labor of love has not gone unnoticed. You are deeply loved and appreciated—not only by hearts you have tended, but by the God who made you the mother (and expert gardener) you are.

*G*od bless you, Mom.

There never was a woman like her. She was gentle as a dove and brave as a lioness.... The memory of my mother and her teachings were, after all, the only capital I had to start life with, and on that capital I have made my way.

—ANDREW JACKSON

CHAPTER TWO

a Mother's Classroom

Your teachings have great importance! What you teach guides your children when they walk and watches over them while they sleep. Your instructions are lights for their lives and speak to them even when you aren't there.

Love,

Your God of Wisdom

Proverbs 6:20–23

You may not have a professional degree, but you are a world-class teacher all the same. And you practice your profession on a daily basis—not on a college campus or behind a podium in a marble-floored classroom—but right there in the warmth of your carefully kept home.

18

While you've gone about the rigorous routines of motherhood, little eyes have watched, and little minds and hearts have been shaped for eternity.

Your young pupils have learned of sacrificial love as they've seen you take the last and least so others can have more. They've learned to distinguish right from wrong as they've observed your life of honesty and integrity.

*T*hey've learned about faith as they've heard you pray to an unseen God— sometimes in tears, sometimes with thanksgiving, always with a firm belief that God is real, that He hears your prayers, and that He responds faithfully.

They've learned that failure is not final as they've seen you confess your own faults and offer generous forgiveness to others.

*A*bove all, they've learned what real love means—it means sharing hurts, hopes, joys, and homecomings; it means staying when it would be easier to leave, defending when others accuse, holding on when you're tempted to let go, and letting go when you desperately want to hold on.

*T*he same lips that
have countless times
formed the word
Mom will say,

"Thanks, Mom, for
your precious teachings.
You're the best."

My mother was the most
beautiful woman I ever saw.
All I am I owe
to my mother.
I attribute all my success
in life to the moral,
intellectual, and physical
education I received from her.

—GEORGE WASHINGTON

If you can't make it better,
you can laugh at it.

—ERMA BOMBECK

CHAPTER THREE

a Mother's Faith

Fan the flame of My gift in your children. Sincere faith can be passed on to your

children and to their children
from generation to
generation. Keep passing on a
heritage of faith. Don't let
My flame go out!
Love,
*Your 100%
Faithful God*

2 Timothy 1:5–6

When it comes to
matters of eternity,
moms have a special
sense. Somehow moms
can see beyond
disheveled hair, freshly
torn jeans, and
smudged faces.

*M*oms can look into
the tearful eyes of an
unhappy two-year-old
or the questioning eyes
of a moody teenager
and see not only what
is—but what can be.

As you interact with your children in your daily routines—routines that may seem mundane and far removed from eternity—remember that you are imparting a sense of something much bigger than the here and now.

*Y*ou are imparting seeds of faith. As your children watch you react to sadness, joy, tragedy, success, and failure, they begin to learn what it means to have faith in something beyond themselves.

Your gentle reassurance when things go wrong, your unfailing confidence in the face of apparent failure, your ability to trust God when life seems to be falling apart—these responses give faith structure and meaning. You are the "embodiment" of faith—faith "with skin on."

*E*very new day presents
opportunities to pass on
little bits of your faith —
little bits of eternity.
Enjoy a beautiful sunset
together and remind your
children of the God who
made it.

When hearts get broken or dreams fall apart, remind them that God holds the key to real happiness and that He is the rebuilder of hopes and dreams. When uncertainty clouds their vision, lead them to their knees in prayer—pray with them often and about everything.

When Satan wins a battle, wrap your arms around them, gently embrace confidence back into them, and tell them of God's unconditional love—a love that will love them no matter what. When it comes to matters of eternity… moms have a special sense.

41

I believe the most valuable contribution a parent can make to his child is to instill in him a genuine faith in God.

—DR. JAMES DOBSON

CHAPTER FOUR

a Mother's Encouragement

*Encourage and build up
your family daily. Help them
identify and get rid of everything that hinders them and the
sin that so easily entangles*

them. Challenge them to run
with endurance the race of life
I've already marked out for
them. Give them courage!

Love,

*Your God Who
Gives You Endurance
and Encouragement*

1 Thessalonians 5:11;
Hebrews 3:13; 12:1; Romans 15:5

A word of
encouragement from
Mom takes the *im* out
of *impossible*, the *'t*
out of *can't*, and the
un out of *unable*.

A cheerful word
from Mom can turn
impending failure
into success and can
spur a child on to
finish a seemingly
impossible task.

This world can be a frightening place—classroom assignments, playground bullies, music recitals, competitive sports—such challenges often require the courage of David facing Goliath.

At times like these,
children—both young
and old—need the gift
of courage. And that's
what *encouragers* do—
they impart *courage*—
and moms are some of
the best encouragers
in the world.

$\mathcal{J}$ust a few simple
words from you give
your children courage
to meet the challenges
at hand:

"I believe in you."
"You can do it."
"You are so special."
"I am so proud of you."
"Keep going…
keep fighting…
keep believing."

This world is full of people and events that drain faith and spirit from your family, but God has given you the ability to fight off these enemies with loving words of encouragement. Never underestimate their power.

*W*atch your children's backs straighten, their eyes brighten, their work improve, their lives change, and their love deepen—all because you have imparted courage to them by your words.

*Every time we encourage
someone, we give them a
transfusion of courage.*

—CHARLES SWINDOLL

CHAPTER FIVE

a Mother's Hope

You are worth far more than rubies! You lack nothing of value. You bring good to every day. You work vigorously, and your life is profitable. You are clothed with strength and dignity! You can laugh at life. You speak with wisdom and faithful instruction; you juggle numerous roles and use your time wisely.

Your children arise and call you blessed, and your husband also praises you! Many women do noble things, but you surpass them all! Others also see what you do and admire your work as a mom.

Love,

Your God Who Praises You for Fearing Me

Proverbs 31:10–30

I have an important
message for you. It
may come as a surprise,
because this message
is not repeated nearly
often enough. Are
you ready?

*Y*ou are greatly
admired. It's
worth repeating.
You are greatly
admired.

*A*nd not just by your family—by others too. Some of your admirers are close acquaintances; others are strangers. But they all hold you in high regard. Why? Because you are a mother through and through, in and out, and all about.

$\mathcal{B}$ecause you are
totally in love with
your family and are
thoroughly prepared
to show your love by
giving all, asking little,
and accepting less.

*B*ecause you have become an expert at being in three places at one time, because you are a tender nurse with a sick child, because you are a diplomatic disciplinarian, because you are a mighty warrior against the forces of evil that threaten your home.

$\mathcal{B}$ecause you see the amazing potential in the hearts and minds of awkward, and sometimes annoying, boys and girls.

*P*lease disregard any previous messages you may have received that gave the impression that you were not highly valued and greatly respected. You are a rich and treasured gift from God.

You may do many other things in your life on earth that will be productive and meaningful, but none will be as admired as being the beautiful mother you are.

*Who ran to help me
when I fell
And would some pretty
story tell,
Or kiss the place to make it
well? My mother.*

—ANN TAYLOR

Look for these other little *Hugs* books:

A Little Book of Hugs for Friends
A Little Book of Hugs for Sisters
A Little Book of Hugs for Women
A Little Book of Hugs for Teachers
A Little Book of Hugs to Encourage and Inspire

Also look for these full-size *Hugs* books:

Hugs for Women
Hugs for Friends
Hugs for Mom
Hugs for Kids
Hugs for Teachers
Hugs for Sisters
Hugs for Those in Love
Hugs for the Hurting
Hugs for Grandparents
Hugs for Dad
Hugs for the Holidays
Hugs to Encourage and Inspire